COURAGEOUS HEARTS

NAVIGATING THE PSYCHOLOGY OF RESILIENCE IN THE BATTLE AGAINST DISEASE

DR ALTON

Copyright © [2024] by Dr Alton

3

Table of contents

Contents

4

Conclusion

Introduction

Trying to Stay Alive: Conquering Infection is a gallant excursion that people leave upon when confronted with imposing wellbeing challenges, like malignant growth. Even with difficulty, this try turns into a demonstration of the human soul's versatility and assurance to win over sickness. The expression "Engaging for Perseverance" embodies the difficult idea of the battle against infection, where people not just wrestle with the actual signs of their condition yet additionally gather inward solidarity to get through the close to home and mental cost.

Infection, especially a conclusion like malignant growth, acquaints a significant interruption with one's life, requiring a diverse way to deal with explore the intricate scene of treatment, recuperation, and individual change. The journey for perseverance suggests a continuous battle, a diligent work to defeat impediments, and a promise to confronting the difficulties with faithful determination.

This fight reaches out past the clinical domain, including way of life changes, profound determination, and a steady organization that all in all structures a hearty starting point for the singular's battle against the sickness. Whether through clinical medicines, way of life changes, or the development of a positive outlook, people participated in this fight endeavor not exclusively to make due yet to arise more grounded, stronger, and significantly different by their excursion.

"Doing combating for Perseverance" is a source of inspiration, encouraging people to bridle their internal strength, look for suitable clinical consideration, and embrace a comprehensive way to deal with prosperity. It recognizes the intricacy of the battle while underscoring the significance of persistence, trust, and the cooperative endeavors of clinical experts, parental figures, and the actual people.

8

In essence, overcoming disease transforms into a metaphorical "battlefield" where the mental, emotional, and spiritual dimensions of endurance are required in addition to the physical. The excursion towards recuperation and mending turns into an account of win over misfortune, a moving story that repeats the unyielding human soul even with life changing difficulties.

Mind study of engaging against sickness.

The mind study of engaging against dangerous development and various disorders is a confusing and dynamic piece of a singular's overall success. Adjusting to a troublesome infection incorporates up close and personal, mental, and social responses that can move exceptionally among individuals. Coming up next are a few significant mental perspectives that are much of the time saw in the battle against malignant growth and different illnesses:

Significant Rollercoaster:

A threatening development finding or any troublesome sickness much of the time sets off an extent of sentiments, including shock, fear, inconvenience, shock, and anxiety. Adjusting to these unprecedented sentiments can be trying, and individuals could experience a fluctuating significant scene all through their trip.

Methods for surviving:

People encourage different methods for surviving to deal with the tension and weakness that goes with a troublesome disorder. Among these are searching out friendly help, rehearsing care, embracing a cheery viewpoint, and utilizing humor as a survival technique.

Versatility and perseverance:

One of the main parts of mental strength is the ability to conquer obstructions and adjust to new circumstances. Various individuals defying disorder display dumbfounding adaptability, finding strength even with trouble and adjusting to the hardships of their new reality.

Inspiration and confidence:

For those engaging sicknesses, developing idealism and hope can be fundamental. Mental prosperity and generally speaking personal satisfaction can be improved by putting stock in the chance of recuperation and zeroing in on the positive parts of life.

Mental Strategies:

Mental procedures incorporate managing examinations and feelings about the infection. This could consolidate reconsidering pessimistic contemplations, setting commonsense suppositions, and cultivating a sensation of control over pieces of life, despite the challenges.

Occupation of Social Assistance:

Social assistance from family, associates and the greater neighborhood tremendously critical. People's ability to adapt to the disease's local weight and overall prosperity can be improved by receiving profound, practical, and enlightening assistance from others.

Course and Fortifying:

People can be helped by effectively participating in clinical navigation and treatment plans. Getting a handle on their decisions, getting explanation on major problems, and collaborating with clinical consideration specialists add to a sensation of control over the situation.

Antipathy for Repeat:

Survivors struggle with a fear of disease recurrence. Managing this fear incorporates advancing correspondence with clinical benefits providers, tending to stresses as they arise, and making methods for adjusting to anxiety about what the future holds.

Significance Making and Reflection:

Various individuals track down significance and reason in their cycle by considering their experiences. This course of significance making can be a wellspring of mental strength and motivation to seek through the challenges of treatment and recovery.

Social-psychological mediation:

People may be given a space to investigate and explore their feelings through psychosocial mediations like directing, support groups, and psychotherapy, for instance. These intercessions address the psychological and significant pieces of the sickness and its impact on everyday presence.

It's crucial to observe that the psychological experience of doing combating against threatening development and ailments is especially individualized. Providers of medical services, doctors, and support groups all play important roles in meeting the various mental needs of people with difficult illnesses. During the most common way of battling sicknesses, coordinating both clinical and mental consideration for complete prosperity is fundamental

Clinical Treatment and Interview:

While managing testing conditions like malignant growth, clinical treatment and interview are fundamental parts of conquering infection. Searching for brief and thorough clinical guidance is the basic beginning stage in arranging a convincing and specially crafted method for managing supervising and vanquishing the illness. Here are focal issues to ponder in the space of clinical treatment and meeting:

Conference speedily:

Early Revelation: Ideal revelation and finding basically impact treatment results. Standard prosperity check-ups and screenings expect a pivotal part in contracting sicknesses, including illness, at an early and more treatable stage.

Customized Care:

Oncologists and Educated authorities: Interview with explicit clinical consideration specialists, similar to oncologists and significant prepared experts, is principal. These experts can give encounters into the possibility of the disease, treatment decisions, and estimate.

Pursuing Choices In light of Information:

Choosing Treatment Options: Patients should successfully attract with clinical benefits specialists to sort out the available treatment decisions.

Individualized Treatment Plans:

Tweaked Approach: Clinical specialists cultivate individualized therapy plans considering factors like the sort and period of the ailment, as a rule, and the patient's tendencies. Adequacy is enhanced and secondary effects are minimized when treatment plans are tailored to the individual.

Open Correspondence:

Convincing Correspondence: Open and direct correspondence among patients and clinical benefits providers is critical. Patients should be able to talk about their worries, get answers to some pressing questions, and effectively participate in treatment decisions.

Clinical Starters:

Examining Exploratory Meds: Dependent upon the specific situation, clinical benefits specialists could look at the possibility participating in clinical starters. Clinical progressions and admittance to state of the art medicines might be made conceivable by these preliminaries.

The executives of Incidental effects:

Directing Auxiliary impacts: For the patient's overall well-being, it is essential to determine the medicines' expected effects and effectively monitor them. Regular communication with healthcare providers enables the ability to make any necessary treatment plan modifications promptly.

Doubts:

Searching for Second Appraisals: Patients hold the choice to search for second sentiments to ensure trust in the proposed treatment plan. This can give additional perspectives and encounters that add to informed autonomous course.

Sweeping Procedure:

Integrative Medicine: A few people might look into integrative medicine, which combines conventional clinical treatments like needle therapy and dietary changes with them. In any case, it's fundamental to work with such techniques with the fundamental clinical benefits bunch.

In investigating the complexities of clinical therapy and meeting, a helpful and informed association among patients and clinical consideration specialists is basic. The establishment for an exhaustive and productive procedure for conquering illness is laid by this organization, which gives people the power to pursue choices that are in accordance with their qualities, inclinations, and in general prosperity.

Changes in way of life:

Lifestyle changes accept a fundamental part in the battle against ailment, especially while facing troublesome sicknesses like dangerous development. While they are not a substitute for clinical prescriptions, these movements can enhance traditional medicines and add to a particular's overall success. Here are key lifestyle changes that individuals should seriously think about:

Dietary Adjustments:

Take on an even and nutritious eating routine that consolidates different regular items, vegetables, whole grains, and lean proteins.

Make a one-of-a-kind meal plan with an enrolled dietitian that meets the individual's specific needs and complements their clinical treatment.

Conventional Real work:

Partake in standard movement as persevered, considering the guidance of clinical benefits specialists. Exercise can help energy levels, further foster outlook, and work on overall real prosperity.

Choose exercises that are appropriate for your level of health, such as gentle strength training, yoga, or strolling.

Adequate Rest:

In order to support the body's normal healing processes, prioritize quality sleep. Establish a loosening up dozing climate and adhere to an ordinary resting plan.

Counsel clinical consideration providers expecting rest aggravations proceed.

Stress Decrease:

Practice pressure lessening strategies like thought, significant breathing exercises, or care to ease up close and personal strain.

Participate in exercises that make you blissful and assist you with unwinding, which will assist you with fostering an uplifting perspective.

Hydration:

Ensure you stay hydrated by drinking sufficient water. Staying hydrated is fundamental for by and large, especially during prescriptions that could cause drying out.

Smoking Discontinuance and Confining Alcohol Affirmation:

Smoking can have a negative impact on your overall health and make treatments less effective.

Limit your liquor admission in light of the fact that, especially during sickness and therapy, unnecessary drinking can adversely affect the body.

Social Assistance:

Foster serious solid areas for an association of buddies, family, and individual patients. Social affiliations offer significant assistance and can positively impact mental success.

Mind-Body Practices:

To help you relax and feel less anxious, look into mind-body strategies like reflection, representation, or directed symbolism.

Ponder essential therapies, similar to needle treatment or back rub therapy, with the heading and underwriting of clinical consideration specialists.

Training and support from here on out:

Stay informed about the specific infection, treatment decisions, and anticipated accidental impacts. Being capable empowers individuals to really partake in their thought.

Advocate for oneself by presenting requests during clinical courses of action and searching for second notions when imperative.

Standard Clinical Check-ups:

Go to arranged clinical plans and screenings as recommended by clinical benefits specialists to screen progress and address any concerns right away.

These lifestyle changes with everything taken into account add to an extensive method for managing prosperity, supporting the solitary's determination in the battle against disease. It's basic for tailor these acclimations to individual necessities and talk with clinical consideration specialists for redid heading.

Emotionally supportive network:

A vigorous emotionally supportive network is a fundamental part in the excursion of doing combating sicknesses like malignant growth. A network of people who offer emotional, practical, and sometimes even medical support is necessary because of the difficulties and ambiguities that accompany a health crisis. This emotionally supportive network assumes a critical part in encouraging flexibility, upgrading the personal satisfaction, and adding to the general prosperity of the singular confronting the illness. Here are key parts of an emotionally supportive network:

Friends and Family:

Consistent encouragement: Friends and family offer a wellspring of profound strength, compassion, and understanding. Their presence can reduce sensations of separation and give solace during troublesome times.

Functional Help: Loved ones frequently step in to assist with day to day undertakings, for example, shopping for food, dinner planning, transportation to clinical arrangements, and childcare.

Medical care Group:

Clinical Direction: The medical care group, including specialists, medical attendants, and care staff, frames a basic piece of the emotionally supportive network. Navigating treatment options, managing symptoms, and comprehending the overall health picture all depend on their expertise and direction.

Support Gatherings:

Peer Association: Joining support bunches permits people to associate with other people who share comparative encounters. A sense of community and shared wisdom can be provided by this shared understanding, which can be empowering.

Data Sharing: Support gatherings can be important wellsprings of data about medicines, methods for dealing with stress, and assets.

Advisors and Therapists:

Profound Prosperity: Emotional well-being experts can give a place of refuge to people to communicate their sentiments, fears, and nerves. Adapting to a difficult disease frequently includes tending to inner difficulties, and these experts offer significant direction.

Local area Associations:

Asset Access: Different people group associations and not-for-profits represent considerable authority in giving assets, monetary help, and pragmatic help for people engaging illnesses. These associations can assist with exploring the mind boggling scene of medical care and deal help customized to explicit requirements.

Otherworldly Help:

Otherworldly Pioneers or Counselors: For those with a strict or profound tendency, looking for direction from otherworldly pioneers can give solace, comfort, and a feeling of direction.

Online People group:

Virtual Help: In the computerized age, online discussions and networks can offer a stage for people to interface, share encounters, and access data. For those who may be restricted geographically, virtual support can be especially helpful.

Working environment backing:

Manager and Partners: Speaking with managers about the wellbeing circumstance and looking for working environment facilities, if necessary, can be significant. Colleagues who are supportive can help create a positive work environment.

An exhaustive emotionally supportive network recognizes the interconnectedness of physical, close to home, and viable necessities. It perceives that confronting a difficult sickness is definitely not a single excursion however an aggregate exertion where every part of the emotionally supportive network assumes an essential part in assisting people with exploring the intricacies of their wellbeing challenges.

Mind-Body Techniques:

Mind-body systems incorporate an extent of practices that perceive the interconnectedness of the mind and body, seeing that mental and near and dear success can influence genuine prosperity. By cultivating congruity between the brain and body, these strategies mean to work on by and large wellbeing. Here are some routinely used mind-body techniques:

Meditation:

Description: Reflection incorporates focusing the cerebrum, much of the time through care or coordinated imagery, to achieve a state of significant loosening up and inspired care.

Benefits: Diminishes pressure, further creates obsession, works on near and dear flourishing, and may insistently impact real prosperity.

Mindfulness:

Description: Care remembers being totally present for the continuous second, seeing contemplations and opinions without judgment.

Benefits: reduces stress, anxiety, and misery, increases concentration, and improves mental well-being in general.

Yoga:

Description: A mix of genuine positions, breathe control, and examination, yoga progresses flexibility, strength, and mental clearness.

Benefits: Deals with genuine health, lessens pressure, overhauls loosening up, and maintains significant harmony.

Kendo:

Description: An old Chinese military craftsmanship depicted by drowsy, streaming turns of events and significant unwinding.

Benefits: improves strength, flexibility, and balance while also reducing stress and fostering calm.

Biofeedback:

Description: a cycle that gives people the ability to control their physiological capabilities by giving them constant input, usually through electronic observation.

Benefits: Regulates conditions like headaches, consistent desolation, and stress-related wrecks by growing care and control over significant responses.

Deep Breathing Exercises:

Description: Various systems incorporate deliberate control of breath to progress loosening up and diminish pressure.

Benefits: Calms the tactile framework, cuts down circulatory strain, and helps in pressure the leaders.

Coordinated Imagery:

Description: Portrayal strategies that incorporate making mental pictures to bring loosening up and good sentiments.

Benefits: Decreases disquiet, further creates outlook, and works on a sensation of thriving.

Moderate Muscle Loosening up (PMR):

Description: a strategy that involves working and relaxing different muscle groups to put real pressure on them and get them to relax.

Benefits: Diminishes muscle strain, eases up tension, and advances a sensation of calm.

Hypnotherapy:

Description: A helpful technique that prompts a shock like state to progress loosening up, concentration, and suggestibility.

Benefits: can be utilized to treat different circumstances, like nervousness the board, propensity the executives, and agony the executives.

Breath-focused Practices:

Description: Strategies, for instance, diaphragmatic breathing or breath care, focusing on the relationship among breath and mental state.

Benefits: Progresses loosening up, diminishes apprehension, and supports overall flourishing.

When facilitated into an expansive wellbeing plan, mind-body procedures can expect a significant part in directing tension, dealing with close to home health, and supporting real flourishing. People frequently discover that these practices enhance their overall quality of life when confronted with health issues.

Teach Yourself

Educate yourself" is areas of strength for a that features the significance of data and care in various pieces of life. Whether applied to insightful pursuits, capable new development, or mindfulness, the possibility of self-preparing highlights the proactive getting of information, capacities, and pieces of information to work on one's appreciation and limits.

With respect to prosperity and success, "Teach Yourself" takes on critical importance, especially while going up against hardships like disorders or infirmities. This incorporates searching for data about the specific burden, sorting out available treatment decisions, and becoming familiar with possible lifestyle changes that can add to taking everything into account. A particularly taught individual can successfully participate in decisions about their clinical consideration, partake in huge conversations with clinical consideration specialists, and patron for their own thriving.

Self-preparing connects past traditional educational settings and embraces a steady, dependable learning approach. It urges individuals to stay curious, research novel ideas, and stay open to different perspectives. With regards to exploring life's intricacies, versatility and strength are fundamental characteristics.

Self-training is now more accessible than ever thanks to the phenomenal access to data provided by computers. Online resources, books, articles, courses, and very capable ends give a wealth of information fit to be examined. Regardless, it's imperative for approach information fundamentally, ensuring its steadfastness and relevance to one's specific prerequisites.

"Educate Yourself" lines up with the likelihood that data is a stimulus for individual reinforcing. By being proactive in acquiring information and capacities, individuals can take care of their lives, make informed decisions, and seek after ways that line up with their goals and values.

Also, the course of self-preparing isn't limited to formal tutoring frameworks; it wraps individual experiences, reflections, and the understanding obtained through trial and error. Embracing a mindset of dependable learning develops mindfulness, flexibility, and a more significant understanding of oneself and the world.

Overall, "Teach Yourself" serves as a core value for those who recognize the revolutionary power of information. It is a call to action to actively seek information, remain curious, and do so in order to continuously strive for personal and collective improvement. Whether applied to prosperity, employment, or personal growth, the commitment to self-preparing opens approaches to extra open doors and ads to a fantastic and connected with life.

Keep an Inspirational perspective:

Keeping an uplifting perspective is a strong and groundbreaking outlook that can fundamentally affect one's process in defeating sickness. While confronting wellbeing challenges, developing an inspirational outlook turns into an encouraging sign, adding to in general prosperity and upgrading the viability of clinical medicines. Keeping a positive outlook is essential for a number of reasons, including:

Improved Versatility:

Inspiration encourages flexibility, permitting people to return from difficulties and face difficulties with reestablished assurance. Flexibility is a vital figure exploring the promising and less promising times of a wellbeing venture.

Stress Decrease:

A positive mentality mitigates pressure, which is indispensable for people managing disease. Stress decrease can emphatically impact the body's capacity to recuperate and answer clinical medicines.

53

Worked on Personal satisfaction:

An uplifting perspective can add to a superior personal satisfaction, even amidst clinical medicines. It permits people to zero in on parts of life past the illness, keeping a feeling of business as usual and bliss.

Enhanced Immune Performance:

Logical examinations recommend an association between a positive mentalities and worked on resistant capability. A well-working insusceptible framework is urgent for the body's capacity to battle sickness and backing the mending system.

Strengthening and Dynamic Interest:

A positive mentality engages people to effectively partake in their treatment plans. It encourages proactive communication with healthcare providers, adherence to prescribed treatments, and a willingness to investigate alternative options to improve one's overall health.

Depression and anxiety reduction:

Energy can assist with easing side effects of discouragement and uneasiness that frequently go with a difficult sickness. It advances a more hopeful perspective on the future and facilitates the close to home weight related with the infection.

Encouraging Strong Connections:

Keeping an uplifting perspective draws in and supports strong connections. Companions, family, and guardians are frequently attracted to the people who ooze energy, making major areas of strength for an organization that assumes an essential part in the recuperating system.

Connection between the Mind and the Body:

The psyche body association is a strong peculiarity. A positive outlook can decidedly impact actual wellbeing, advancing recuperating and recuperation.

Motivation and Optimism:

Inspiration energizes trust and inspiration, fundamental components for getting through a difficult wellbeing venture. Trusting in the chance of recuperation can move people to drive forward through troublesome times.

Production of a Mending Climate:

An inspirational perspective adds to the making of a mending climate, both intellectually and inwardly. This can decidedly impact the body's reaction to treatment and backing by and large wellbeing.

Basically, keeping an inspirational perspective isn't tied in with denying the difficulties of sickness yet about deciding to zero in on the conceivable outcomes, qualities, and wellsprings of delight that can coincide with the excursion toward recuperating. A proactive and enabling decision can significantly influence the direction of defeating illness.

Monitoring and checks on a regular basis:

Normal check-ups and observing assume a urgent part in overseeing and defeating illnesses, particularly persistent or difficult circumstances like disease. There are several reasons why regular medical follow-ups are necessary:

Early Discovery:

Customary check-ups work with the early identification of any progressions or complexities connected with the sickness. Early distinguishing proof permits medical services experts to intercede quickly, possibly further developing therapy results.

Modification of treatment:

Healthcare professionals are able to evaluate the efficacy of ongoing treatments thanks to monitoring. Based on the patient's response and any new developments, the treatment plan can be modified if necessary.

Counteraction and Hazard The board:

Normal check-ups help in observing potential gamble elements and entanglements related with the illness. Medical care experts can give direction on preventive measures and hazard decrease methodologies to upgrade generally speaking prosperity.

Management of Symptoms:

Illnesses frequently accompany a scope of side effects, and standard check-ups give an open door to medical services suppliers to successfully address and deal with these side effects. During treatment, this may enhance the patient's quality of life.

Management of medications:

Checking guarantees appropriate administration of prescriptions. Medical services experts can evaluate the requirement for changes in measurement or changes in medicine in view of the patient's condition and any secondary effects experienced.

Psychosocial Assistance:

Check-ups offer a stage for patients to examine their profound and mental prosperity. Medical care suppliers can interface patients with suitable psychosocial support administrations or directing, tending to the all encompassing parts of wellbeing.

Patient Instruction:

Ordinary checking gives an open door to medical care experts to instruct patients about their condition, therapy choices, and way of life alterations. Informed patients are better prepared to take part in their consideration effectively.

Preventive Screenings:

Occasional screenings and tests, as suggested by medical care suppliers, can help with the early identification of likely difficulties or optional circumstances connected with the illness.

Long haul Care Arranging:

Constant checking upholds the improvement of long haul care plans. As the patient's condition develops, medical services suppliers can work with patients to lay out sensible assumptions and objectives for their continuous consideration.

Laying out Trust and Correspondence:

Normal check-ups add to the foundation of a trusting and open connection among patients and medical care suppliers. This supports successful correspondence, taking into consideration the trading of data and worries that are pivotal for extensive consideration.

It is fundamental for people to stick to the suggested timetable of check-ups and observing framed by their medical services group. Patients and healthcare professionals benefit greatly from this collaborative approach to disease management, improved treatment outcomes, and improved overall health and well-being.

Hydration and Smoking Suspension:

Hydration and smoking end are two urgent way of life factors that fundamentally influence generally speaking wellbeing, particularly while engaging illnesses like disease. Both contribute significantly to the body's capacity for healing and recovery. Here is a more critical gander at the significance of hydration and smoking end with regards to defeating sickness:

Hydration:

Cell Capability and Recuperating:

Satisfactory hydration is fundamental for cell capability, digestion, and the body's regular recuperating processes. It upholds the vehicle of supplements and oxygen to cells, working with by and large wellbeing.

Treatment Incidental effects The executives:

Hydration can assist with overseeing results of specific clinical medicines, like chemotherapy, by flushing out poisons and advancing kidney capability. It might mitigate side effects like exhaustion and queasiness.

Resistant Framework Backing:

Patients undergoing treatment need to drink enough water to help their immune systems function properly. A very much hydrated body is better prepared to fight off diseases and sicknesses.

Stomach related Wellbeing:

Hydration supports keeping up with solid absorption, forestalling difficulties, for example, obstruction that might emerge during specific clinical medicines.

Energy Levels and Essentialness:

Keeping hydrated helps you feel more alive and energetic. This is especially significant for people confronting the weariness frequently connected with sickness and therapy.

Temperature Guideline:

Drinking enough water helps keep the body's temperature in check, which is important for people who have a fever or other temperature changes caused by treatment.

Stopping Smoking:

Upgraded Treatment Viability:

Stopping smoking can improve the viability of clinical medicines. Smoking is known to disrupt the body's reaction to medicines, and end further develops generally treatment results.

Diminished Treatment Intricacies:

Smoking discontinuance can decrease the gamble of entanglements during and after clinical intercessions. It advances better twisted mending, diminishes the gamble of diseases, and upgrades the general outcome of surgeries.

Cardiovascular Wellbeing Improvement:

Smoking discontinuance essentially works on cardiovascular wellbeing. This is critical for people managing disease, as a solid cardiovascular framework upholds the conveyance of oxygen and supplements all through the body.

Diminished Treatment Aftereffects:

Stopping smoking can mitigate specific treatment incidental effects. For instance, people going through radiation treatment might encounter less respiratory issues assuming that they stop smoking.

Lower Hazard of Auxiliary Diseases:

Smoking suspension brings down the gamble of creating optional sicknesses, for example, cardiovascular infections and respiratory difficulties, which can be especially inconvenient to people previously managing a difficult disease.

Worked on By and large Prosperity:

Stopping smoking adds to worked on in general prosperity. It upgrades lung capability, increments energy levels, and emphatically influences psychological wellness, factors that are fundamental for people exploring the difficulties of ailment.

A true holistic approach to health includes, in essence, drinking enough water and quitting smoking, especially when overcoming a serious illness. These way of life decisions support the body's actual strength as well as add to a general climate helpful for recuperating and recuperation. It is prudent for people to talk with their medical services experts for customized direction and backing in carrying out these changes.

Clinical Starters:

Clinical starters expect a pivotal part in pushing clinical data, developing new treatments, and further creating results for individuals standing up to various sicknesses, including illness. Patients may gain access to cutting-edge medicines and contribute to advancements in clinical science by participating in clinical preliminary studies. Here are key perspectives to consider concerning clinical starters:

Investigation and Improvement:

Clinical fundamentals are at the extreme forefront of clinical assessment and headway. People can add to the improvement of new treatments, therapy approaches, and clinical information that can help future patients by taking part in a preliminary.

Permission to Exploratory Meds:

New and exploratory medicines that probably won't be accessible through standard consideration are habitually accessible through clinical preliminaries. This can be particularly basic for individuals who have exhausted standard treatment decisions.

Personalized Method of Care:

Various clinical starters intend to survey zeroed in on or altered treatment moves close. Participating in such starters could offer individuals prescriptions that are redone to the specific ascribe of their disorder, perhaps provoking more victories.

Close Noticing and Care:

Individuals in clinical starters draw near checking and care from a multidisciplinary clinical benefits bunch. This can work on the idea of care and deal additional assist all through the treatment with cycling.

Obligation to Consistent Data:

People gain a deeper understanding of the components of a disease and the effects of treatment by participating in clinical preliminary studies. This information is principal for refining and making future treatment frameworks.

Various Choices:

For specific individuals, especially those with confined treatment decisions, clinical starters can address an elective street for conceivable helpful interventions. It opens up extra open doors past standard medications.

Trust and Reinforcing:

Support in clinical fundamentals can bestow a sensation of trust and reinforcing. It licenses individuals to successfully partake in their treatment cycle and add to types of progress that could end up being useful to others in tantamount conditions.

Moral Oversight and Patient Prosperity:

In order to ensure the well-being of patients, clinical preliminary procedures are run under strict moral guidelines and administrative oversight. Individuals are instructed about the probable risks and benefits, and their opportunities are protected all through the primer.

78

Multidisciplinary Joint exertion:

Clinical primers incorporate joint exertion among clinical consideration specialists, experts, and individuals. This multidisciplinary approach supports a sweeping perception of the sickness and its therapy, perhaps provoking additional convincing therapies.

Induction to Solid Associations:

Individuals in clinical starters regularly become piece of a consistent neighborhood individuals standing up to near prosperity challenges. Everyday reassurance, shared encounters, and helpful data can be generally given by this organization.

Talking with their medical team, fully understanding the goals, potential risks, and benefits of the preliminary, and making an informed decision in light of their particular condition are crucial for people considering support in clinical preliminary. Clinical fundamentals hold the responsibility of impelling clinical science and offering expect additionally created treatment results for individuals doing battling ailments like dangerous development.

Conclusion

n end, the excursion of fighting against infections, particularly impressive enemies like disease, is a complex and profoundly private experience that incorporates physical, close to home, and mental aspects. From the snapshot of determination, people set out on a way that requires versatility, flexibility, and a comprehensive way to deal with prosperity. All through this difficult excursion, a few key components arise:

The significance of an inspirational perspective couldn't possibly be more significant, as it fills in as a directing light, encouraging strength, decreasing pressure, and adding to a general feeling of prosperity. Keeping up with confidence isn't tied in with denying the weightiness of the circumstance yet deciding to zero in on conceivable outcomes, qualities, and wellsprings of satisfaction in the midst of difficulty.

Customary check-ups and observing structure a significant part of sickness the executives, offering open doors for early identification, therapy change, and preventive measures. Predictable clinical subsequent meet-ups, combined with open correspondence with medical services experts, make an establishment for far reaching care and backing.

Hydration and smoking discontinuance stand apart as

fundamental way of life decisions that altogether influence the body's capacity to recuperate and recuperate. Appropriate hydration upholds cell capability and invulnerable wellbeing, while at the same time stopping smoking works on cardiovascular wellbeing as well as upgrades the viability of clinical medicines.

The consideration of clinical preliminaries in the battle against sicknesses gives an encouraging sign and a road for getting to noteworthy therapies. Cooperation in preliminaries offers likely advantages to people as well as adds to propelling clinical information, molding future medicines, and building a steady local area.

The brain science of engaging infections mirrors the perplexing transaction of feelings, survival techniques, and individual versatility. Navigating the journey's psychological difficulties requires adapting one's coping mechanisms, seeking out social support, and accepting a variety of emotions.

Basically, beating sicknesses is an all encompassing undertaking that requires a cooperative exertion from medical services experts, people, and their encouraging groups of people. It includes the joining of clinical medicines, way of life changes, mental help, and a positive outlook. The excursion is set apart by achievements, misfortunes, and snapshots of significant thoughtfulness, at last molding the story of versatility, trust, and the victory of the human soul over affliction. As people face the vulnerabilities of their wellbeing process, the aggregate endeavors of the clinical local area, steady organizations, and the person's own solidarity meet up to enlighten a way toward mending, recuperation, and a reestablished feeling of prosperity.